STEM!
TECHNOLOGY
EDITED BY
MARZIA TEMPOLI
LIGHTBOX
openlightbox.com

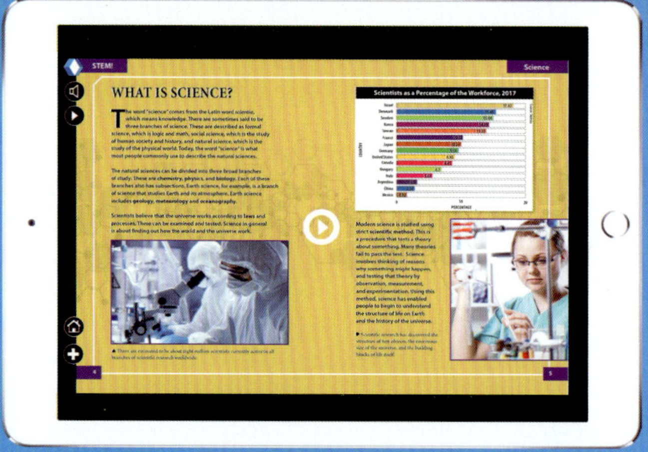

Lightbox is an all-inclusive digital solution for the teaching and learning of curriculum topics in an original, groundbreaking way. Lightbox is based on National Curriculum Standards.

STANDARD FEATURES OF LIGHTBOX

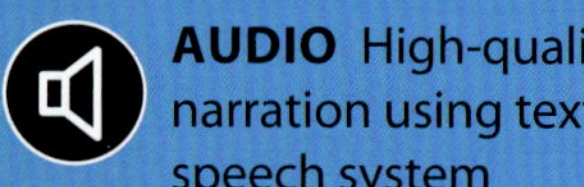

AUDIO High-quality narration using text-to-speech system

ACTIVITIES Printable PDFs that can be emailed and graded

SLIDESHOWS Pictorial overviews of key concepts

VIDEOS Embedded high-definition video clips

WEBLINKS Curated links to external, child-safe resources

TRANSPARENCIES Step-by-step layering of maps, diagrams, charts, and timelines

INTERACTIVE MAPS Interactive maps and aerial satellite imagery

QUIZZES Ten multiple choice questions that are automatically graded and emailed for teacher assessment

KEY WORDS Matching key concepts to their definitions

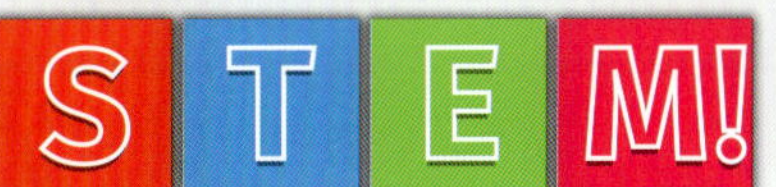

TECHNOLOGY

CONTENTS

WHAT IS TECHNOLOGY?

Technology is the practical use of scientific knowledge. Technologists are scientific inventors who look at how scientific principles and processes can be used to make useful tools and machines. For example, a scientist may discover that mixing lime, clay, and gypsum will produce a substance that will stick things together. A technologist may show how this substance can be used to build a brick wall. A civil **engineer** will then work out how to make buildings using this new technology of bricks and mortar.

Modern technology is built on advances made in technology over previous decades. Cell phones evolved to become the smartphone of today. Other technologies developed to replace existing technologies. Steam-powered trains were once the new transportation technology. Today, superfast electric trains reduce journey times, as well as air pollution. Technology has led to inventions that make it easier for people to travel and communicate. It has improved homes and lifestyles. Computers have made it possible to collect and analyze data more efficiently. They have enabled school and college students to learn more effectively.

The jet engine enabled airplanes to travel faster and carry heavier loads.

In hospitals, groundbreaking developments in the treatment and care of sick patients have been made possible by technological advancements in surgical machines and equipment. However, some people point to the disadvantages of technology. Job losses, personal security issues, and increasingly destructive weapons of war are reminders that technology is a tool that can be used for better or for worse.

Technology in the 2020s

It is hard to predict the technologies that will dominate the next decade. However, some of those that exist today may play a key role.

Technology	Applications	Problems
Quantum Sensors are very small devices that can make precise measurements.	In medical science, quantum sensors are used for brain imaging, detecting early signs of heart disease, and monitoring cancer treatment. They can also be used to map underground structures such as remains of ancient cities.	None, although some quantum sensors are expensive to create.
Artificial Intelligence (AI) is the use of computers to identify patterns of data.	AI can make many decisions presently made by individuals, such as medical diagnoses or screening applicants for jobs.	Many people are worried about computers making decisions that affect people's lives.
Robots are machines that can be programmed to carry out many tasks.	Robots can carry out repetitive tasks such as cleaning or working on a production line.	It is estimated that 20 million jobs worldwide could be lost to robots in the next decade.
Electric Cars are automobiles that are powered by electricity, rather than gasoline engines.	Electric cars could cut exhaust emissions in large cities and lessen the dependence of modern societies on polluting substances such as gasoline and oil.	The batteries that store electricity in electric cars hold a limited charge, and recharging takes considerable time.
Drones are vehicles that can be controlled and sent to their destination by remote control.	Drones are already used extensively by the military. In the future, they could be used to deliver goods in civil society.	Controlling independent drone operators is difficult. They could pose a danger to aircraft or people if flown by irresponsible people.

TECHNOLOGY WORLDWIDE

More than three million years ago, people began to use simple stone tools. By about 50,000 years ago, people were also making small tools such as needles from bone. The invention of the potter's wheel between 6000 and 4000 BC in Mesopotamia enabled people to make pots from clay. People used these pots to carry water for use in their homes. Pots were also used as containers for food. The **shaduf,** invented in ancient Egypt, made it possible for farmers to water their fields efficiently. In the Middle Ages, China was the source of many innovations, including the invention of gunpowder and the magnetic compass.

In Europe in the 1800s, the **Industrial Revolution** was a time of great technological development. The process carries on to this day. By the twenty-first century, digital technology was transforming the world.

San Francisco, United States
In 1977, the Apple II, Commodore PET, and TRS-80 computers were presented at the West Coast Computer Faire in San Francisco. These were the first personal computers. The Faire was the start of the personal computer industry.

Nile Delta, Egypt
The shaduf was first used in about 2000 BC. It was used by ancient Egyptian farmers to lift water from rivers, lakes, or streams. The water was poured into trenches cut in the fields to irrigate or water the crops.

Arctic Ocean
Coalbrookdale, Great Britain
Abraham Darby invented a way of using coal to produce iron. This was the basis of the Industrial Revolution that began in Europe in the 1700s.
Mannheim, Germany
In 1886, Karl Benz patented the first automobile powered by an internal combustion engine. This engine was the basis for the worldwide automobile industry.
Atlantic Ocean
EUROPE
ASIA
Pacific Ocean
AFRICA
Indian Ocean
AUSTRALIA
Olduvai Gorge, Tanzania
Stone tools dating back millions of years were found in the Olduvai Gorge. This is the oldest known evidence of technology in the ancient world.
MAP LEGEND
Land
Water
N
SCALE
0
1,000 miles
1,000 kilometers
Southern Ocean
ANTARCTICA

The Ancient and Medieval World

The first civilizations began about 5,000 years ago. From then to the start of the Industrial Revolution in the 1700s, the technology people used improved, but only gradually. People made weapons, buildings, and clothing from wood, stone, and other natural materials.

The basis of these technologies had been developed centuries earlier. People had known how to use fire for hundreds of thousands of years. About 20,000 years ago, they learned how to shape and bake clay from the earth in ovens to make waterproof pots. Pottery vessels meant people could carry water and store water and foods. People also used fire to separate metal from rocks. They used the metal to make tools. During this long period of history, there were several improvements in technology. The ancient Romans used **concrete** for building houses and roads. Blacksmiths made steel by adding small amounts of carbon to iron.

The remains of pottery artifacts in ancient Egypt, such as in the Valley of the Kings, show how important pottery technology was in the ancient world.

HORSES AND TECHNOLOGY

Horses were fast and strong. People used them in agriculture, commerce, and warfare from prehistoric times. From about 700 BC, the saddle came into use. This enabled people to ride a horse more easily. Before the invention of the saddle, most horses had been used to pull carts, rather than being ridden. Then, in the first three centuries AD, tribes north of China invented stirrups. Before the use of stirrups, balancing on a horse had been difficult. Stirrups meant that heavily armed soldiers, such as knights in armor, could now ride horses. By about 1000 AD, the horse collar had been invented and was in widespread use. The collar allowed a horse to pull three times as much weight as before.

Horses played a vital role in farming during the medieval period.

Tools and weapons were all made by hand. People or animals were the only source of power. People invented ways of increasing the effect of muscle power by inventing machines such as the wheel. This allowed heavy loads to be moved more easily.

The medieval period lasted from about 400 AD to the 1400s. Two important technologies to emerge late in the period were gunpowder and printing. Warfare became very different as a result of gunpowder weapons. With the invention of the printing press in the mid-1440s, books could be printed in large quantities. Ideas and information spread quickly.

All medieval blacksmith's forges had a brick hearth into which air could be blown through bellows. Air made the fire burn hotter, so metal could be heated and softened.

The Industrial Revolution

The Industrial Revolution that began in Great Britain in about 1760 and lasted until about 1880 was a period of great technological advancement. People burned coal and **coke** to produce higher temperatures than could be achieved by burning wood. The heat produced by coal was used to drive machines called steam engines. Smelting, a process involving heating and melting, was used to produce iron and steel.

The new availability of large amounts of iron and steel led to significant changes in all aspects of technology. Machines were invented that could do work previously only done by hand. In 1733, John Kay invented the flying shuttle, which allowed weavers to produce cloth wider than the arm's reach. Then, in 1801, the weaving loom was invented. This meant that fabric could be woven much faster than had been possible by hand. In 1831, the mechanical reaper machine was invented by Cyrus McCormick in the United States. This could do the work of five people in cutting cereal crops. The age of **mass production** had begun. This marked a shift in society. People who had once lived and worked in the countryside moved to the cities to find work. They were employed in factories.

Cotton mills were factories that employed workers of all ages to turn raw cotton into cloth.

The huge machines that produce iron and steel in the modern world would have been unimaginable to people before the Industrial Revolution.

The Industrial Revolution changed the way people looked at the world. This period is sometimes called "the invention of invention." If a new scientific theory was proposed, inventors started to think about how they could make practical use of it. In 1876, the inventor Thomas Edison opened the first research laboratory at Menlo Park in New Jersey. Teams of inventors worked on thousands of new inventions, including the phonograph and the electric light bulb.

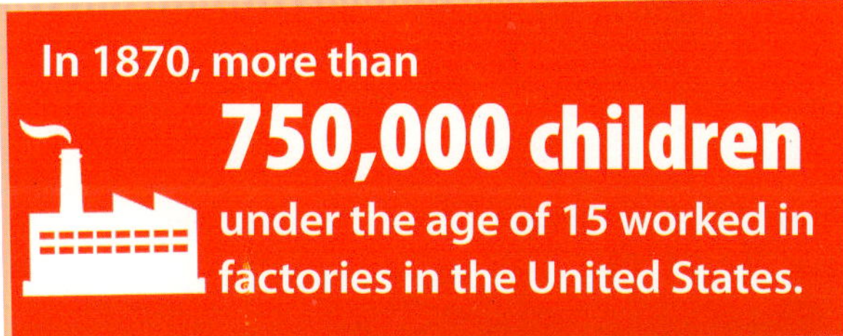

By 1850, more than **50 percent** of the population of Great Britain lived in towns and cities.

In 1870, more than **100,000 steam engines** were at work in Great Britain.

Looking at Transport and Flight Technology

In the Industrial Revolution, steam engines that could run on rails were invented. At the same time, steam began to be used to power ships. These ships had steel hulls and engines, rather than wooden hulls and sails. The first steamships were propelled by a large paddle wheel on the side of the ship. By the mid-1800s, the paddle wheel was replaced by a propeller at the rear of the ship.

By the late 1800s, the internal combustion engine was invented. This technology led to the invention of the automobile and powered flight. The internal combustion engine was also critical for the modern automobile industry. The first car was built in 1885 by Karl Benz.

The Wright Brothers designed and flew the first successful powered airplane. They carried out their experiments in Kitty Hawk, North Carolina.

Other technologies, such as the invention of rubber tires, then made the automobile more comfortable. Automobiles powered by the internal combustion engine have lasted for more than a century. A worldwide industry constantly making innovations has grown up around the internal combustion engine. Today, however, companies are developing cars powered by electricity.

Engine-powered flight was first achieved by the Wright Brothers in 1903. The Wright Brothers controlled the machine in the air by making adjustments to the angles of the wings and propeller. The technology developed by the Wright Brothers paved the way for airplane design that lasted for more than 30 years. Today, a whole new class of airplane engines has been developed. These are powerful jet engines that can reach greater speeds than ever before.

Most of today's large container ships are powered by a large single diesel engine. They are driven by a propeller.

JET ENGINES

Until the late 1930s, all airplanes were pulled through the air by propellers driven by a version of the car's internal combustion engine. During World War II, however, a different form of propulsion was tested. This was the jet engine. In modern jet engines, air is drawn into the engine. It mixes with aviation fuel and is ignited. The resulting hot gas is forced backward out of the engine, which pushes the aircraft forward. Jet engines are now the most common types of engine. They are used for both civilian and military aircraft.

The large fans at the front of a jet engine draw in air to mix with the aviation fuel.

Looking at Military Technology

Throughout history, technology has been developed quickly during times of war. In the 1600s, many countries were at war. Italian scientist Galileo Galilei worked out the path a cannonball might take through the air. This began the science of ballistics, or the study of how missiles such as bullets fly. A further advance was when military scientists developed more accurate weapons, using a technology called **rifling**. This involved carving spiral grooves down the inside of a gun barrel, causing the bullet to spin when it came out. A spinning bullet flies in a straighter, more accurate line.

During the 1800s, more powerful guns were developed that could be fired over longer distances. The shells they fired became more destructive. Then, in 1884, the machine gun was developed. This was an **automatic weapon** that could fire a number of bullets with one pull of the trigger.

Modern tanks such as the Abrams are equipped with the latest military technology. This includes machine guns, rifled guns, armor plating, and computerized firing systems.

The machine gun was invented by American inventor Hiram Maxim. Machine guns changed the nature of warfare. Their rapid rates of fire caused many deaths and injuries.

The next development in military technology was to make machines that could carry the new deadly weapons. Tanks and aircraft were built, and metal armor that could protect them was invented.

By 1945, scientists had worked out how to split atoms. This released huge amounts of energy. Atomic bombs were dropped on Japan at the end of World War II in 1945. These bombs were by far the most powerful and destructive weapons ever used in warfare.

▲ Modern military aircraft carry bombs, missiles, and automatic weapons. The aircraft cost many millions of dollars to manufacture.

A .50 inch machine gun can hit targets from a distance of up to **7,382 feet** (2,250 meters).

A modern M134 machine gun can fire at a rate of **6,000 rounds** of bullets per minute.

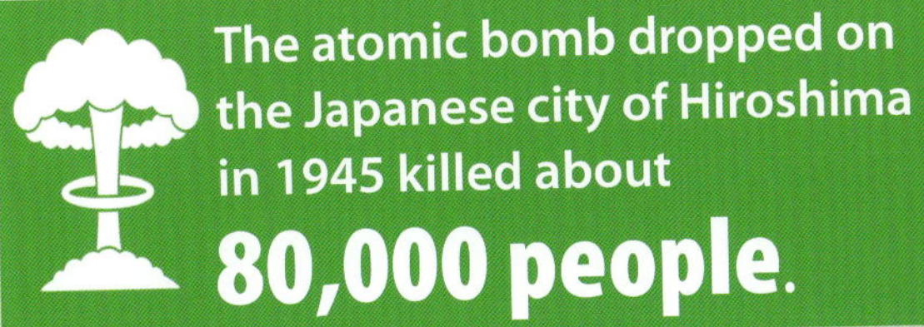

Looking at Electricity, Communication, and the Home

In the late 1800s, a new form of power became readily available. This was electricity. People had known about electricity for centuries, and in the early 1800s, scientists such as Michael Faraday had worked out how to make and control electricity in laboratories. In 1879, electric light bulbs were first used to light a street, and the first electric power station came into use in 1891. Batteries, the first one made by Alessandro Volta in 1800, made electricity portable.

Electricity was not only used for lighting. Using electrical wires, messages could be tapped out in **Morse Code**. Cables were laid across the ocean floor and international communication became possible. Alexander Graham Bell won the first U.S. **patent** for the electric telephone in 1876.

In 1895, Guglielmo Marconi worked out how to communicate using radio waves. Radio waves are a series of peaks and valleys. The pattern before it repeats itself is called a cycle. Radio waves are picked up by a receiver and converted into mechanical vibrations in a speaker to create sound waves.

The bright lights of cities such as New York are powered by electricity.

TELEVISION

In 1921, Edouard Belin sent the first image using radio waves. By 1926, improved radio wave receivers meant that Scottish scientist John Logie Baird was able to send moving images. The technology relied on reproducing an image using 30 lines of information. The invention of the **cathode ray tube** made it possible to send more lines of information. Color images began to be sent in the 1930s, using a system of red, green, and blue filters. By 1941, 525 lines were being sent. These gave a much sharper image. By the 1980s, almost all TV programs were in color. The first TV images sent via a **satellite** were broadcast in 1962.

Early TV sets had a long body to house the cathode ray tube, which provided the black and white pictures on the screen.

Electricity and radio waves form part of the **electromagnetic spectrum**. Light from the Sun is in the middle of this spectrum. Invisible radio waves are at the low end of this spectrum.

Electricity became the major source of power in the 1900s. Instead of driving steam engines, coal was used in power stations to create electricity. All the major devices used by people today are driven by electricity. Homes are lit by electric light. Food is kept cool in electric refrigerators. Cell phones are powered by electric batteries. Electricity is the most important technology in the modern world.

The working parts of a light bulb are designed so that the electric current can flow quickly and easily.

Looking at Computers and Digital Technology

The ways that people could use electricity in all sorts of machines changed in the middle of the twentieth century. New inventions such as **transistors** meant that electrical equipment could be made smaller. This paved the way for the age of information technology (IT).

Transistors can be manufactured cheaply. They can be put together to form **integrated circuit** boards (ICB) that occupy a small physical space. Each transistor has to perform a single, simple function, but because there are so many transistors on the circuit board, they can combine to undertake something complicated such as driving a computer.

The first ICB was created by Jack Kilby in 1958. Since then, technology has developed to enable the production of smaller transistors, which in turn enables ICBs to be used in smaller devices.

Modern electronic devices are powered and controlled by integrated circuits. Sometimes known as microchips, these are usually made from silicon and contain many tiny transistors. Silicon does not conduct electricity very well in its pure state. However, it can be treated to make it conduct more electrical charges. Silicon also resists heat and does not break down under intense electrical activity.

Over the past 50 years, electronic components have grown smaller. At the same time, integrated circuits have become more powerful. They control everything from cars to toasters and coffee machines.

Integrated circuits also enabled scientists to invent modern computers. The first computers had been extremely large. Some filled entire rooms. Then, in 1977, the first personal computers that could sit on a desktop were presented at the West Coast Computer Faire in San Francisco. The speed with which transistors and integrated circuits were made smaller and more powerful led to new generations of small laptop computers, and in turn to modern cell phones and tablets. These devices make contact worldwide via communications satellites that orbit Earth.

The smartphone is a small computer. It can receive and transmit radio waves. Early computer pioneers would be astonished at the power of this tiny device, and how little it costs.

The money spent on IT and computers annually worldwide is estimated at **3.8 trillion dollars.**

There are **2,134** communications satellites in Earth's orbit.

China has **800 million** Internet users, India has 700 million, and the United States has 275 million.

TIMELINE OF TECHNOLOGY

Many of the people who developed technology in the ancient and medieval world are unknown. This all changed with the start of the Industrial Revolution in the 1700s. Inventors and their inventions changed the way the world worked. Technology drove economic growth. Today, governments and multinational companies spend large budgets on developing new technologies to improve the lives of people in the future.

8700 BC | **2000 BC** | **1000 AD** | **1450** | **1750**

3500 BC
Wheels are used to pull carts and other farm vehicles.

8700 BC
Copper tools and jewelry are made in what is now Iraq.

750 AD
Stirrups are invented for horseback riding in Europe.

1455
Johannes Gutenberg prints the Bible on a printing press with moveable type that can be reused.

1800
Alessandro Volta creates the first electric battery. Volta uses zinc and copper plus sulfuric acid or saltwater.

1895
Guglielmo Marconi transmits and receives radio-wave signals.

1926
The first electronic transistor is patented.

2018
A self-driving car completes a 485-mile (780-km) journey from Moscow to Kazan.

1800 **1850** **1900** **2000** **2019**

1834
Cyrus McCormick is granted a patent for his reaping machine.

1939
The Heinkel company makes the first aircraft powered by a turbojet engine.

QUIZ

ONE
What is a shaduf?

TWO
Where were gunpowder and the magnetic compass invented?

THREE
What invention allowed horses to pull three times more weight?

FOUR
What did Abraham Darby develop at Coalbrookdale?

FIVE
What is rifling?

SIX
When was the machine gun invented?

SEVEN
What was used to light streets in 1879?

EIGHT
What powers the lights of modern cities such as New York?

NINE
How were TV images broadcast in 1962 for the first time?

TEN
What material is most commonly used for making microchips?

ANSWERS

ONE A device for raising water in a bucket to irrigate fields **TWO** China **THREE** The horse collar **FOUR** A way of using coal to make iron **FIVE** Cutting grooves into the barrel of a gun to make the bullets fly straighter **SIX** 1884 **SEVEN** Electric light bulbs **EIGHT** Electricity **NINE** By satellite **TEN** Silicon

KEY WORDS

automatic weapon: a weapon that fires a stream of bullets with one pull of the trigger

cathode ray tube: a tube, usually made from glass, that allows electrons to display an image on a screen

coke: coal that has been heated in special ovens and burns at very high temperatures

concrete: a building material using cement mixed with gravel or sand

electromagnetic spectrum: the whole range of radiation and light in the universe

engineer: a person who builds or maintains machines and structures

Industrial Revolution: the developments in technology and manufacturing that began in the 1700s

integrated circuit: a group of transistors set on a single piece of silicon, or microchip

internal combustion engine: an engine that drives machines by igniting gasoline in an enclosed chamber to operate pistons

mass production: the production of identical goods in large quantities, usually in factories by machines

Morse Code: a system of electronic communication using dots, dashes, and spaces for letters and numbers

patent: the legal recognition that someone has invented something new

rifling: grooves that make a bullet spin when it is fired

satellite: a small object that orbits, or revolves, around a larger object in space

shaduf: a bucket on the end of a moveable pole used to water fields

transistors: small electronic devices that can amplify a signal

INDEX

LIGHTBOX

SUPPLEMENTARY RESOURCES

Click on the plus icon found in the bottom left corner of each spread to open additional teacher resources.

- Download and print the book's quizzes and activities
- Access curriculum correlations
- Explore additional web applications that enhance the Lightbox experience

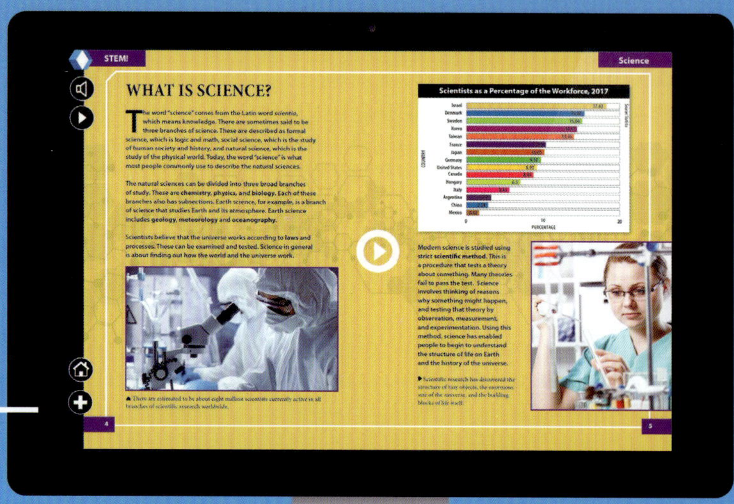

LIGHTBOX DIGITAL TITLES
Packed full of integrated media

VIDEOS

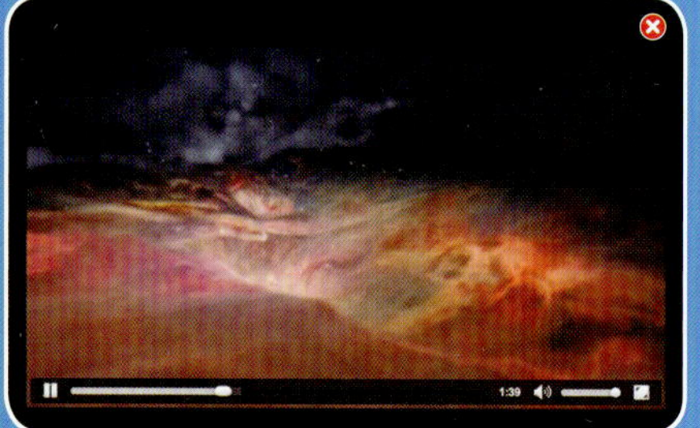

INTERACTIVE MAPS

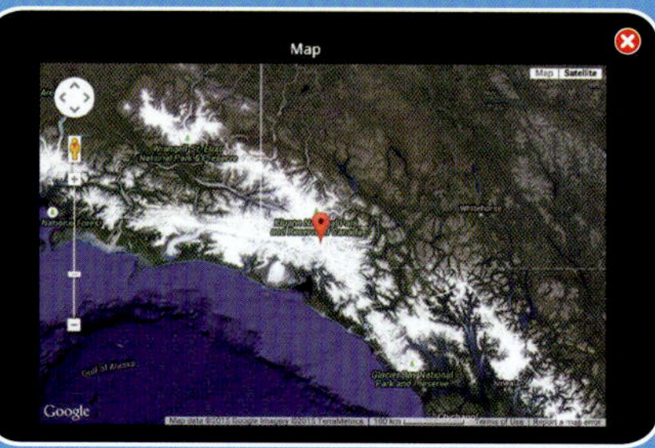

WEBLINKS

SLIDESHOWS

QUIZZES

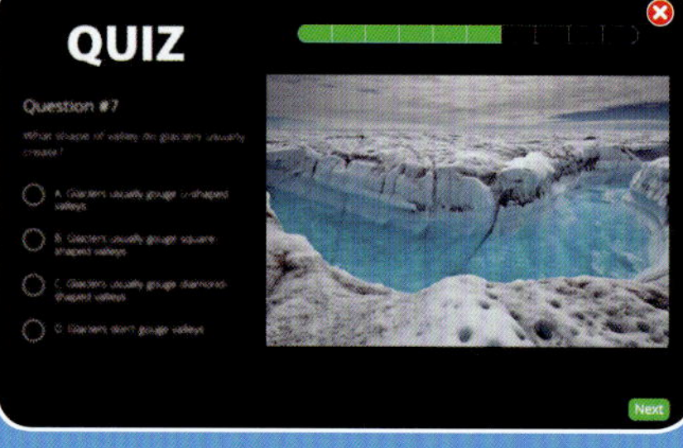

OPTIMIZED FOR
- ✓ TABLETS
- ✓ WHITEBOARDS
- ✓ COMPUTERS
- ✓ AND MUCH MORE!

Published by Smartbook Media Inc.
350 5th Avenue, 59th Floor New York, NY 10118
Website: www.openlightbox.com

Project Coordinator: Heather Kissock
Art Director: Terry Paulhus

Library of Congress Control Number: 2019942197

ISBN 978-1-5105-4413-0 (hardcover)
ISBN 978-1-5105-4414-7 (multii-user eBook)

Printed in Guangzhou, China
1 2 3 4 5 6 7 8 9 0 23 22 21 20 19

072019
121819

Photo Credits
Every reasonable effort has been made to trace ownership and to obtain permission to reprint copyright material. The publisher would be pleased to have any errors or omissions brought to its attention so that they may be corrected in subsequent printings.

The publisher acknowledges Alamy, Shutterstock, and Wikimedia as its primary image suppliers for this title.